Surrender to Love

Featuring Come to the Fire Testimonies on DVD
by Anne Lowe, Kikky Williams,
Tracey Goss, and Linda Boyette
With Journal Bible Studies by Aletha Hinthorn

This book is intended for both small group and individual reading.

To order this book, go to www.cometothefire.org.

Library of Congress Cataloging in Publication Data:
ISBN 978-0-9800033-0
Printed in the United States of America

10 9 8 7 6 5 4 3 2 1

All Scripture quotations not otherwise designated are taken from the Holy Bible, New International Version (NIV). Copyright © 1973, 1978, 1984 by International Bible Society. Used by permission of Zondervan Publishing House.

Permission to quote from the following additional copyrighted versions of the Bible is acknowledged with appreciation:

The Amplified Bible, Old Testament (AMP), copyright © 1965, 1987 by Zondervan Corporation. The Amplified New Testament (AMP), copyright © 1954, 1958, 1987 by The Lockman Foundation.

The Holy Bible, New Living Translation (NLT), copyright © 1996. Used by permission of Tyndale House Publishers, Inc., Wheaton, IL 60189. All rights reserved.

The King James Version (KJV), copyright © 1963 by Finis Jennings Dake. Dake Bible Sales, Inc., Lawrenceville, GA 30246. All rights reserved.

Table of Contents

Week Three: Find True Life

Week Four: Surrender to Love

Introduction

Come to the Fire presents you with small group Bible studies using testimonies given at the conferences by Anne Lowe, Kikky Williams, Tracey Goss, and Linda Boyette.

We suggest that for discussion of the homework, the group (if larger than eight or ten) break into smaller groups to discuss the studies.

Each leader could pre-select topics and questions that seem appropriate to ask the group from that week's homework. Allow the Spirit to guide the discussion.

Small Group Suggestions

To encourage accountability, we suggest the following ideas for discussion. The leader of each group could ask the woman on her left the three questions below. After answering, that woman would ask the same three questions to the person sitting on her left, and so on around the circle.

• What did Jesus say to you from His Word and your study this week?

• How have you applied this Word to your daily life?

• How can we pray for you?

Our love increases as we pray for each other (Philippians 1:7-9). Not only that, healing came to Job when he prayed for his friends (Job 42:10). What a beautiful concept—healing comes to our hearts as we pray for one another!

If a woman is not prepared, she could simply say, "I must pass today. Would you please pray for me?" And right then the one asking for her accountability will lift her in prayer.

The measure of prayer for the group will determine the measure of the Spirit you enjoy. And "when he, the Spirit of truth comes, he will guide you into all truth" (John 16:13).

5

Day 1
Refining Moments

Today's Focus from Anne Lowe: God used refining moments in my life.

Cricket Albertson, granddaughter of Mrs. Dennis Kinlaw, wrote the following paragraphs about her grandmother who lived a life of prayer. She described several decisions her grandmother made early in life that helped shape her Christian life. Such moments of decision can be both refining and defining moments that shape our future with the Lord. Mrs. Kinlaw's decisions still bless her children, grandchildren and many others today.

"Several weeks after meeting Jesus, Elsie was bouncing down her dormitory stairs, and looked out a window. At that moment, she heard Jesus whisper, 'You have given me your heart; would you give me your whole life?' Her answer characterized every other answer she would ever give to Him: 'Oh, Jesus, Yes!'

"After that, Elsie's life was marked by a passionate love for Jesus, for people, and for service. Those commitments Elsie made to Jesus determined every other decision she made, and became the cornerstone for all that Jesus would do with her life.

"One of the most impressive achievements to me, her granddaughter, was how she kept her first love. I want to know the secret of her surrendered life. I think she had three ways to maintain her love relationship with Jesus Christ.

"First, she sought His presence. She found delight in spending time with Him, and she insisted on that time. If she had any spare moments, she would go into a quiet corner and begin to talk to Jesus. He was her relaxation and her strength.

"Second, she listened to the Holy Spirit's voice. When He whispered to her heart, she immediately obeyed. As a result of this listening heart, she chose to separate herself from anything that contained a taint of sin. For instance, when she was a young bride, she was staying with her family while her new husband was preaching. She said that she heard the Holy Spirit whisper to her not to spend her evenings watching TV, so when her family watched television she would sneak upstairs, work on a scrapbook, and pray for her new husband who was out telling people about Jesus.

"In decisions like this, apparently small decisions, the pattern of her life was set. Not recreation first, not Elsie first, not family first, but Jesus first. The rest of her life, she consistently prayed through the hours when her husband was preaching. She had established her choice of Jesus first long before. She was willing to live without anything as long as she had Jesus.

"Finally, she never let anything come between her and her first love. If she felt she had offended Christ in any way, she immediately asked for His forgiveness. She was even free to ask for others' forgiveness if she felt she had spoken in haste! She lived her life with a clean heart and with a passionate commitment to let the Holy Spirit keep it clean."

Our Refining Moments

We often set our course by seemingly small resolutions. What were decisions Mrs. Kinlaw made that helped determine the direction of her future?

"I made haste, and delayed not to keep thy commandments" (Psalm 119:60). Opportunity to obey is often like a horse that comes galloping by and pauses. If we fail to get on, it gallops away, taking our opportunity to ride with it. A glimpse of how we can follow God more closely may be with us only long enough for us to decide if we'll obey it or disregard it.

In the following references, what were the decisions made that affected generations to come?

Abraham (Genesis 22:2)

Joseph (Genesis 50:15-21)

Judas (Matthew 26:14-16)

After the twelve spies returned from exploring Canaan, only Joshua and Caleb reported that because God was with them they could conquer the land. Notice that according to Numbers 14:24, the reward was not only to Caleb himself. Who else was blessed?

Consider how carefully obeying each of the following verses could make a difference in not only your life but also the lives of others, even future generations. What could be some rewards of obedience and also what could be consequences of ignoring these commands?

"So put to death the sinful, earthly things lurking within you. Have nothing to do with sexual immorality, impurity, lust, and evil desires. Don't be greedy, for a greedy person is an idolater, worshiping the things of this world" (Colossians 3:5 NLT).

"Make allowance for each other's faults, and forgive anyone who offends you. Remember, the Lord forgave you, so you must forgive others" (Colossians 3:13 NLT).

"Get rid of all bitterness, rage, anger, harsh words, and slander, as well as all types of evil behavior" (Ephesians 4:31 NLT).

Scripture for Meditation

"Teach us to number our days aright, that we may gain a heart of wisdom" (Psalm 90:12).

"But seek first his kingdom and his righteousness, and all these things will be given to you as well" (Matthew 6:33).

"Reflect...for the Lord will give you insight" (2 Timothy 2:7). What insights do you get from these verses? How will you apply them?

Journaling Time

Space to think, write, pray, and hear God

What decisions have you made in the past that you now recognize to be defining or refining moments? Were there opportunities for obedience (or disobedience) to God that have become significant moments for you?

Day 2
Love Like Jesus!

Today's Focus from Anne Lowe: I was amazed how my vision had changed; I was looking at them with the perfect love Jesus had given me.

The most searching passage in the New Testament is 1 Corinthians 13:4-7 that describes the love we are to express to others. But divine love, *agape*, is not something we do, but something we have. It is God within us who is doing the loving. The controlling verb is "have."

In this study, each of the phrases from these verses in 1 Corinthians 13:4-7 is quoted from two or more versions.

Divine Love Described

1. "Love endures long and is patient and kind" (Amp.).

"This love is slow to lose patience—it looks for a way of being constructive" (Phillips).

Hatred prompts harshness, but love tends to make us gentle, tender, and affectionate.

Impatience and irritability are among our most common temptations. Would you agree with this statement: "There is no more sure sign of a disciplined mind than a habit of tolerant patience?" Why or why not?

2. "Love never is envious nor boils over with jealousy" (Amp.). "Love is not possessive" (Phillips).

We tend to be envious of those most like ourselves. A housewife might be envious because someone else's home is nicer or another mother's kids are more popular. What situations tempt you to envy? What does jealousy say about satisfaction with God's provision.

3. "[Love] is not boastful or vainglorious, does not display itself haughtily" (Amp.). "It is neither anxious to impress nor does it cherish inflated ideas of its own importance" (Phillips).

Love "does not show off." It does not do its "acts of righteousness" so others will notice and be impressed. According to Matthew 6:1, what are the results of trying to impress others by our good deeds?

4. "[Love] is not conceited—arrogant and inflated with pride" (Amp.). "It is not proud" (NIV).

It's free from what was a vice in the Corinthian church (1 Corinthians 4:6, 18, 20; 5:2; 8:1). How does the statement Paul made in 1 Corinthians 4:7 help us to maintain humility?

5. Love (God's love in us) does not insist on its own rights or its own way, for it is not self-seeking" (Amp.). "Love has good manners and does not pursue selfish advantage" (Phillips).

Love isn't "me first" but seeks to make others happy. See Romans 15:1-2. What are the benefits of building others up?

See this demonstrated in Paul in 1 Corinthians 10:33. Compare it to Philippians 2:20. Have you experienced this demonstration of love?

6. "[Love] is not touchy or fretful or resentful" (Amp.). "Love is not irritable" (NLT).

Perfect love rises above all temptations to be resentful or angry although it may often be justly indignant. What is the difference between carnal anger and righteous anger?

7. "Love takes no account of the evil done to it—pays no attention to a suffered wrong" (Amp.). "It does not keep account of evil or gloat over the wickedness of other people" (Phillips).

"Love keeps no record of wrongs" (NIV).

What are steps we can take to ensure that we are not keeping track of those who have wronged us?

8. "[Love] does not rejoice at injustice and unrighteousness, but rejoices when right and truth prevail" (Amp.).

"Love does not delight in evil but rejoices with the truth" (NIV).

The Greeks used the term "malignant joy" to describe "rejoicing at the misfortune of others." La Rochefoucald confessed, "There is something not altogether disagreeable to us in the misfortunes of our best friends."

According to Proverbs 24:17-18, what will happen if we rejoice because another has trouble?

Notice that in 1 Timothy 1:3-6, Paul warns Timothy not to become involved in certain kinds of controversies. How would obeying this command promote love? Are there things we should not discuss in certain situations because it might hinder fellowship?

9. "[Love] beareth all things (KJV). "Love knows no limit to its endurance, no end to its trust, no fading of its hope; it can outlast anything. Love never fails" (Phillips).

Love takes the best and kindest views of all people and all situations as long as it is possible to do so.

10. "[Love] hopeth all things" (KJV). "[Love] is always hopeful" (NLT).

Hope is more than the result of a sanguine temperament; it is a gift and a grace. Hope takes the sunny and cheerful view of life.

11. "[Love] endureth all things" (KJV).

"[Love] endures through every circumstance" (NLT).

Love endures the seventy times seven offenses (Luke 17:4). See Paul's own example in 2 Timothy 2:10.

Scripture for Meditation

"Love is patient, love is kind. It does not envy, it does not boast, it is not proud. It is not rude, it is not self-seeking, it is not easily angered, it keeps no record of wrongs. Love does not delight in evil but rejoices with the truth. It always protects, always trusts, always hopes, always perseveres" (1 Corinthians 13:4-7).

"Above all, love" (1 Peter 4:8).

"Reflect...for the Lord will give you insight" (2 Timothy 2:7). What insights do you get from these verses? How will you apply them?

Journaling Time

Space to think, write, pray, and hear God

Sometimes we pray for deliverance when God is saying, "Trust Me to give you sufficient grace and strength for this day." Consider what situation you want to see changed but in which God may be saying, "Trust Me for grace to love unconditionally."

Day 3
The Word Is Alive!

Today's Focus from Anne Lowe: Once Jesus filled all my heart, the Bible became the living Word of God.

Ann Preston, also known as "Holy Ann," was a simple Irish lady who lived nearly 100 years ago. Ann's education began and ended in little more than a week, but in that time she exhausted the patience of the teacher to the point of despair. After many vain attempts to teach her the first letters of the alphabet, he gave her a significant tap upon the head as he remarked before the class, "Poor Ann! She can never learn anything." And with this she was sent home in disgrace. That was the end of her education.

A godly Mrs. McKay hired her, and while working for her, Ann prayed earnestly to have her sins forgiven. She said, "I felt something burning in my heart." She went over to the table and picked up a Testament and, putting her finger on a verse, prayed, "O Lord, You that has taken away this awful burden, intolerable to bear, couldn't you enable me to read one of these things?" The text was, "Whosoever drinketh of this water shall thirst again, but whosoever drinketh of the water that I shall give shall never thirst."

For the first time in her life Ann was able to read. Later, when she yielded absolutely to the Lord and was filled with His Spirit, she made out another verse. Eventually Ann could read her Bible anywhere and everywhere. The most remarkable thing, however, was that Ann was never able to read any other book.

Once a friend put a newspaper before Ann, and she tried her to decipher some of the smaller words. Finally, she put her finger on one word and said, "That seems to be 'lord,' but I don't think it is my Lord, as my heart doesn't burn while I see it." It was a report that spoke of Lord Roberts' achievements.

The words in Scripture are supernatural words with life in them. "The words I have spoken to you are spirit and they are life" (John 6:63). "They are not just idle words for you—they are your life" (Deuteronomy 32:47). "For the Word that God speaks is alive and full of power" (Hebrews 4:12 Amp.). The word translated "full of power" means power in action. The Word, then, is not merely potential power. It is God's power in action. It is doing His work.

God's Word at Work

God's Word has power to cleanse. Perhaps you are not reaping the blessings of having godly parents. Instead, tendencies such as divorce, fear, lying, anger, or use of alcohol or drugs have been passed down from a previous generation to you. Fortunately, patterns of previous generations can be reversed through God's Word. In Jesus' final recorded prayer, He prayed, "Sanctify them by the truth; your word is truth" (John 17:17). Earlier He had told His disciples that they were "clean because of the word" (John 15:3). To gain cleansing through the Word from the iniquities passed down from previous generations, follow these steps.

a. Identify your problem. One mother said she discovered she was angry with her child just as her mother was angry with her when she was little. She did not want to pass this tendency on to her daughter. What tendency do you have that you want God to cleanse from your life?

b. Find a Scripture that states God's desire regarding this disposition or inclination in your life. Trust the Holy Spirit to guide you to His exact truth for your specific need. Ask God for insight and discernment into the root issues of your problem. The following suggestions may help in your search for His Word of cleansing for you.

Anger: Ephesians 4:31-32; Colossians 3:8-12

Fear: 2 Timothy 1:7

Lying: Ephesians 4:25; Colossians 3:8-10

c. "Let the Word of Christ dwell in you richly" (Colossians 3:16). Memorize the Word. Meditate on it. Journal your thoughts as you consider what the verses would look like if applied in your life. "Be made new in the attitude of your minds" (Ephesians 4:23). What will set you free according to John 8:32?

d. Determine that through Christ's strength you will obey the Word. The Lord will enable you to do all He asks you to do in Galatians 5:16, 25. State these verses in your own words.

e. Trust that as you determine to obey Scripture, God can and will enable you to live a life of holiness. Remember that God's limitless power is available to us to change our lives.

f. Apply faith in the blood of Jesus Christ. When Adam sinned in the Garden of Eden, in essence, he said, "Not Your will, but my will be done." Jesus, the second Adam, won back our ability to choose God's will in another Garden, when He said, "Not my will, but yours be done" (Luke 22:42). Claim the power available to you through Jesus' blood. Personalize 1 John 1:7 inserting your need.

g. Determine that with God's supernatural power helping you to obey His Word, you will change your thinking and your habits. Write Ephesians 3:20 in your own words inserting what you are trusting God to do for you.

Scripture for Meditation

"Now ye are clean through the word which I have spoken unto you" (John 15:3 KJV).

"You have purified yourselves by obeying the truth" (1 Peter 1:22).

"Reflect...for the Lord will give you insight" (2 Timothy 2:7). What insights do you get from these verses? How will you apply them?

Journaling Time

Space to think, write, pray, and hear God

Consider what verses the Holy Spirit has used to change your thinking or behavior. How has the Word encouraged, challenged, corrected, or warned you?

Day 4
Live the Word

Today's Focus from Anne Lowe: Once Jesus filled all my heart, the Bible became the living Word of God.

At the close of one of my first days teaching at the Kansas School for the Blind, a fellow music teacher stood at the door of my studio and said, "You seem to be having a better start to your teaching than I did."

"Tell her you prayed about it," the Spirit whispered.

Oh, but I don't know her well enough, I thought and dismissed the idea.

Later, I realized that what I had done was a habit. I wanted with all my heart to do God's will, yet I frequently ignored His promptings.

One night in tears I laid my failures before the Lord. How could I ever change? The Spirit gently spoke these words to my spirit: "You need to learn to obey Me."

I arose from prayer with a new resolution. I knew that obeying God meant obeying His Word. I began to come to

Scripture with a new heart hunger. The next morning when I opened the Bible I was eager to obey the words I read, and I approached the Word differently. No longer was reading routine. It's one thing to be curious about what Scripture says; it's another to hunger for our lives to reflect the truth in the words.

John Wesley said we are to read the Word with "a fixed resolution to do it." This resolve became the key to my new approach to Scripture. I had an inner hunger to obey. What did this passage say about my actions or attitudes? How could I apply this verse? I read with anticipation.

Finding Life in the Word

C. S. Lewis commented that if we would observe the way our physical needs are met, we'd realize that God also prepares pleasant ways for our spiritual needs to be met. What do John 15:11 and 1 John 1:4 say about God's intention for His words to give us joy?

Since His Word is to give us joy, on the mornings when we've awakened with a lack of joy, the cure may be to begin memorizing verses and filling our minds with Scripture. Try having verses on cards available when you get dressed. What are other practical ways you can fill your mind with the Word?

A lady told me, "I bought a Bible because I was hungry." Few people understand that our deepest longing for joy is quenched with God's truth. Instead, they accept Satan's substitutes for joy which are short-lasting and in the end, empty. Solomon called all these efforts to obtain joy "meaningless." Following our own passions leads to death, but learning and doing the will of our Father leads to life.

Samuel Logan Brengle, a favorite preacher in the early days of the Salvation Army, formed a habit of choosing a text for his day. As a traveler stuffs snacks in his pockets, Brengle daily stuffed the pockets of his mind with tasty treats from the Word. These snacks were short, simple statements of promise, reassurance, or comfort he would turn to for support and power along the way.

"Feed on Him in your hearts by faith" is a phrase frequently used in communion services. Develop the habit of keeping nourishing bits of truth readily available and learn to feed on those. Scriptures written on cards to read and obey throughout our day can become "real food" and "real drink" to our spirits.

What benefits of God's Word are mentioned in the following verses?

Psalm 119:45

Psalm 119:98-100

Psalm 119:165

1 Timothy 4:15

John 15:3

Joshua 1:8

Psalm 1:2, 3

The mindset with which we approach God's Word should be like Daniel's who set his mind to gain understanding. (Daniel 10:12) Peter wrote, "Prepare your minds for action; be self-controlled" (1 Peter 1:13).

We must determine to give our whole attention to what we read and refuse to chase every thought that beckons. What are some of the hindrances you experience when trying to read Scripture?

How would you apply Matthew 7:7 and Proverbs 6:6-11 to your Bible reading and study?

Ezekiel is commanded to eat the scroll which is God's Word. He finds it to be as sweet as honey (Ezekiel 3:1-3). See Ezekiel 3:4.

The assimilation of God's Word makes it part of our lives. Why is consuming God's Word important for parents? Consider Deuteronomy 6:6-7.

"Let the word of Christ dwell in you richly" (Colossians 3:16). It takes more than diligent Bible study to have His Word dwelling in us. See John 5:37-38.

Being teachable is the prime prerequisite to finding life in the Word. "Harden not your hearts" was written to Christians. What are evidences that our hearts are pliable enough to be changed by the Word?

Scripture for Meditation

"My son, if you accept my words and store up my commands within you, turning your ear to wisdom and applying your heart to understanding, and if you call out for insight and cry aloud for understanding, and if you look for it as for silver and search for it as for hidden treasure, then you will understand the fear of the LORD and find the knowledge of God" (Proverbs 2:1-5).

"Reflect...for the Lord will give you insight" (2 Timothy 2:7). What do each of these phrases tell us to do? How will you apply them?

Journaling Time

Space to think, write, pray, and hear God

Do you long to have a deeper love for the Word? If you do, express your desire to God in writing. Allow Him to show you how to make His Word more a part of your daily life. What is He saying to you?

Day 5
Pray the Word

Today's Focus from Anne Lowe: My Bible reading and prayer became alive.

"So many of my prayers for my children get in a rut. I pray the same thing day after day," a friend said. "Well, not exactly," she added. "One morning I'll pray, 'Do something today, Lord, to make them think about You.' Then the next morning I pray desperately, 'Don't let anything happen to them today.' It's almost as though I cancel out yesterday's prayers."

Is there some way we can discern what requests to make? How can we know we're asking God to supply exactly what He sees we need?

God has provided two ways for us to discern what requests we should bring to Him. First, He has given us prayers in Scripture that teach us the kind of requests that please Him. Second, He gives us the Holy Spirit to guide our praying. In this chapter, let's consider the impact praying Scripture will have and then discuss ways to turn God's Word into prayer.

Scripture-Inspired Prayers

Paul encourages us to pray taking "the sword of the Spirit, which is the word of God" (Ephesians 6:17). The Old Testament gives examples of such praying. For instance, Daniel spoke to God boldly because he knew what God had said. He "understood from the Scriptures" that the end of Israel's captivity was drawing near. Then he "prayed to the Lord" (Daniel 9:2, 4), and God answered.

The Holy Spirit anointed Paul to know how to ask for things that would produce spiritual maturity. Praying Paul's requests will bring similar results in those for whom we pray.

1. Which phrases from each of the following passages would you like to have someone pray for you? Consider these to be prayers you can pray for others.

Ephesians 1:17-18

Ephesians 3:16-19

Philippians 1:9-11

Colossians 1:9

2 Thessalonians 1:11

Philemon 6

What are themes in these prayers of Paul?

How will others mature spiritually when God answers these petitions?

You may want to make a list of Scriptures you can turn into prayers, such as the following:

Help him (her) to be joyful always; pray continually, and to give thanks in all circumstances recognizing that this is God's will for him (her) in Christ Jesus (1 Thessalonians 5:16-18).

Help him (her) to never tire of doing what is right (2 Thessalonians 3:13).

Help him (her) not to rely on himself but on God (2 Corinthians 1:9).

Make all grace abound to him (her), so that in all things at all times, having all that (s)he needs, (s)he will abound in every good work (2 Corinthians 9:8).

What Scriptural admonitions would you like to see fulfilled in another's life? Write out two of those in the form of prayers.

1.

2.

Are there promises God has helped you to believe regarding others? Put these promises into the form of prayers.

When Jesus said that not one jot or one tittle of His Word would pass away until all is fulfilled (Matthew 5:18), it was as though He said not one dot of the "i" or one curve of the "a" from Scripture will disappear until it is all accomplished. "...not one smallest letter nor one little hook [identifying certain Hebrew letters] will pass from the Law until all things [it foreshadows] have been accomplished" (Amp.).

God promises, "I am watching to see that my word is fulfilled" (Jeremiah 1:12). "The eyes of the Lord keep watch over knowledge," He assures us in Proverbs 22:12.

Because God personally sees that His Word accomplishes His desires, why not use His Word in our prayers? We can reverently quote it back to Him confident that His Word always achieves the purpose for which He sends it. (Isaiah 55:11).

How does Mark 13:31 assure us of the reliability of His Word?

Scripture for Meditation

"So shall my word be that goes forth from my mouth; it shall not return to me empty, but it shall accomplish that which I purpose and prosper in the thing for which I sent it" (Isaiah 55:11).

"Reflect...for the Lord will give you insight" (2 Timothy 2:7). What does this verse teach? How will you apply this verse?

Journaling Time

Space to think, write, pray, and hear God

"The gospel...is the power of God" (Romans 1:16). How has God's Word brought the presence and the power of God into your prayer life?

Day 1
Listen for His Voice

Today's Focus from Kikky Williams: The Word of God was the strength of my life.

Carole had certain expectations for her spiritual life. One was that she should spend some time each morning reading the Bible and saying a prayer. She was faithful in meeting these goals, but half the time she didn't know what she was reading and her prayers were empty. "I hadn't been meeting God. I had been meeting a habit," she admitted.

Then the Holy Spirit taught her to come expectantly in the spirit of Psalm 119:18: "Open my eyes that I may see wonderful things in your law."

Carole reports, "Now when I study the Bible and pray, I come before the Lord expecting that He will have something to teach me. I spend more time listening for His voice instead of getting caught up in my own meaningless words."

She began to ask the Lord to show her a WT (Wonderful Thing) for the day. Instead of reading a set number of chapters each day, she reads a verse or a paragraph, but she reads it meditatively, purposefully, with open ears so God can speak to her.

God Gives Insights

If we want God to reveal "wonderful things" to us in Scripture, we must say as Moses said when he saw the burning bush, "I will now turn aside and see" (Exodus 3:3 KJV). The more we "turn aside" to see, the more God will reveal Himself to us. Sometimes our understanding does not come immediately. It requires time, reflection, and obedience.

Most of all, it requires the inspiration of the Spirit. The Bible is the only book that comes with a Guide, so let's invite the Holy Spirit to speak as we read. D. L. Moody remarked, "The Bible without the Holy Spirit is a sun-dial by moonlight."

How is God's truth revealed to us according to Matthew 16:17 and 1 Corinthians 2:9, 10, 14?

In what ways did your Bible reading change after you became a Christian?

If we do not seek to understand, what happens? See Matthew 13:19.

Of what value is our hearing according to Matthew 13:23?

In Mary's song in Luke 1, she exclaimed, "He has filled the hungry with good things but has sent the rich away empty" (vs. 53). I have come to believe that this can apply to our Bible reading. When we come to the Word hungry to hear a Word from God, He fills us. But if we come thinking we already know all it says, that we're rich with truth, we find nothing. What helps you to come to your Bible reading "hungry?"

"All my longings lie open before you, O Lord" (Psalm 38:9).

A notebook and pen beside our Bibles as we read can become one of the ways we say "Lord, I am expecting to receive something too good to forget." Often fresh insights come as we "turn aside to see" by writing down a verse.

God instructed the king to do more than simply read the Law: "When he takes the throne of his kingdom, he is to write for himself on a scroll a copy of this law" (Deuteronomy 17:18). The process of writing truth would be more profitable to the king than merely reading it, just as it is for us. Why is this true?

Recording what we've read also insures we are more likely to recall those words. One study showed that when we transition from being a passive listener to an active listener by doing something such as picking up a pencil and writing down what we've learned, our retention changes from 10 percent to 40 percent.

Maybe you think, "My ideas aren't worth recording." But if we are faithful to record those one-cent ideas, He will trust us with silver dollar ones. Jesus' words apply:

"Whoever can be trusted with very little can also be trusted with much" (Luke 16:10).

When David was giving his son Solomon the instructions for the temple he was to build, he said, "All this...the Lord made me understand in writing by his hand upon me" (I Chronicles 28:19 KJV). I understand this verse to say that as David wrote, the Lord gave him understanding. I've discovered that is often the process. New insights come as I write down a verse, perhaps because writing slows me down so I can consider carefully each detail. Recording what I'm reading becomes my way of saying to God, "I'm looking to You to teach me what I should hear You say through this verse today." He responds to this desire.

What has helped you in the past to receive new insights?

When Jesus' talked with the two men on the road to Emmaus, they were enjoying the conversation too much to want it to stop. What did they do and what did Jesus do? Read Luke 24:28-32.

A request for understanding pleases God. Luke 24:45 gives one of the final things Jesus did for His disciples. "Then he opened their minds so they could understand the Scriptures." Turn this into a prayer you can pray before reading the Word.

Scripture for Meditation

"Pay attention to what I say; listen closely to my words...for they are life to those who find them" (Proverbs 4:20, 22).

"How sweet are your words to my taste, sweeter than honey to my mouth" (Psalm 119:103).

"Wise men lay up knowledge" (Proverbs 10:14).

"Reflect...for the Lord will give you insight" (2 Timothy 2:7). What insights do you get from these verses? How will you apply them?

Journaling Time

Space to think, write, pray, and hear God

Wisdom is sensitive to who loves her. She calls out, "I love those who love me" (Proverbs 8:17), and sends us ideas. If we love them, welcome and embrace them, she'll send us more. But if we allow them to float away, like bubbles a child blows, their source will dry up. What are ways you can welcome and embrace God's Words? What is God saying to you?

Day 2
You Can Hear Him Speak

Today's Focus from Kikky Williams: The Word came up off the page.

When my husband Daniel was about to begin his third year of medical school, we knew he would have to be on call at night, sometimes leaving me alone as often as every third night. I was terrified to stay alone. We began praying that I would not be afraid those nights he had to stay at the medical center.

The first night Daniel was on call, I happened to open to Proverbs and read, "When thou liest down, thou shalt not be afraid: yea, thou shalt lie down, and thy sleep shall be sweet" (3:24 KJV). I believed God was giving me that as a promise, and those words proved to be absolutely true. When I would lie down, I was not afraid. One night I heard a noise outside, and, remembering my verse, I hurriedly hopped in bed. I was not afraid and went right to sleep.

Sometimes God does speak to us like that, but a better habit is to read according to a routine and expect the Lord to give us what we need in that passage. One day I was desiring God's blessing in a certain situation and wondered if I should fast breakfast and lunch. I knew the Spirit would lead me. In morning devotions our daughter read Psalm 37, and I took the phrase "Wait on the Lord" as my answer. I would fast to tell the Lord I was waiting on Him.

The next morning I opened to Isaiah thinking, I really haven't been getting much out of these chapters. I was tempted to skip to another book but stuck to reading Isaiah. When I came to 25:9, I knew God had this special promise there for me that day: "Lo, this is our God; we have waited for him, and he will save us: this is the Lord; we have waited for him, we will be glad and rejoice in his salvation."

In both of these incidents, God's Word became *rhema* to me. There are two primary Greek words that describe Scripture that are translated *word* in the New Testament. The first, *logos*, refers principally to the total inspired Word of God and to Jesus, Who is the living Logos.

The second primary Greek word that describes Scripture is *rhema*. It refers to a word that is spoken and means "an utterance." A *rhema* is a verse or portion of Scripture that the Holy Spirit brings to our attention with application to a current situation or need for direction.

God's Word to You

Rhema is the revealed Word of God. It comes as an utterance from God to our heart by the Holy Spirit just as He promises to do in John 14:26. Write this verse in your own words.

The following passages give examples of Scriptures that refer to the *logos* of God:

"In the beginning was the Word [*logos*], and the Word [*logos*] was with God, and the Word [*logos*] was God" (John 1:1).

"The seed is the word [*logos*] of God" (Luke 8:11).

"Do your best to present yourself to God as one approved, a workman who does not need to be ashamed and who correctly handles the word [*logos*] of truth" (2 Timothy 2:15).

"For the word [*logos*] of God is living and active" (Hebrews 4:12).

When the Holy Spirit illuminates a particular Scripture, He intends it for application in our daily walk with the Lord. When God gives such a word, a *rhema*, it is a word for us to act on.

How does Jesus speak of *rhema* in Matthew 4:4 and John 6:63?

How do the following passages of Scripture provide insight into the *rhema*s of God?

"Consequently, faith comes from hearing the message, and the message is heard through the word [rhema] of Christ" (Romans 10:17).

"Take the helmet of salvation and the sword of the Spirit, which is the word [*rhema*] of God" (Ephesians 6:17).

"Husbands, love your wives, just as Christ loved the church and gave himself up for her to make her holy, cleansing her by the washing with water through the word [*rhema*]" (Ephesians 5:25–26).

"If you remain in me and my words [*rhema*] remain in you, ask whatever you wish, and it will be given you." (John 15:7).

In the regular course of your daily reading of God's Word (*logos*), ask God to speak to you and give you insight into it. The Holy Spirit can cause certain passages to stand out with significant meaning or application for your life. These are the *rhemas* of Scripture and should become a part of your daily thoughts and actions.

"Those whom I love, I reprove and discipline," the Lord promises Christians in Revelations 3:19. Then He adds, "I stand at the door and knock."

When God knocks on a certain area in our lives by highlighting a Word, it becomes our *rhema*. We have a choice of either submitting to His discipline or refusing.

The Holy Spirit does not speak in generalities. When He gives us a specific word, we will be blessed if we believe it and obey.

Scripture for Meditation

"Were not our hearts burning within us while he talked with us on the road and opened the Scriptures to us?" (Luke 24:32).

"Blessed is the man who listens to me, watching daily at my doors, waiting at my doorway. For whoever finds me finds life and receives favor from the LORD" (Proverbs 8:34-35).

"Reflect...for the Lord will give you insight" (2 Timothy 2:7). What insights do you get from these verses? How will you apply them?

Journaling Time

Space to think, write, pray, and hear God

What Scriptures have been *rhema* to you? How did they impact your life?

Day 3
God's Plans for You Are Perfect

Today's Focus from Kikky Williams: God has the whole plan.

"Play something for me," directed Professor Spector at my first piano lesson at Pittsburg State. I launched into parts of Beethoven's *Sonata Pathetique*. I say "parts" because my previous piano teacher had wanted two of her students to play the sonata at her recital, so she had divided it between us.

About midway through, he abruptly stopped me. "Why are you playing only parts of this sonata?" he demanded.

I explained about the recital and the need to cut parts here and there.

The professor began pacing the floor, irate because of the musical atrocity I had committed. "Do you realize that chopping a Beethoven sonata is like whacking away on a fine painting?" he said, pointing to a picture on his wall.

He was right. A master painter has a purpose for every brush stroke just as a good composer or author never inserts irrelevant details. That's what we expect from human creators, yet we sometimes accuse our loving Creator of allowing irrelevant, insignificant periods in our lives. However, Ephesians 2:10 says that we are God's *poema*—the Greek word for poem, a literary form in which every word is placed with exacting preciseness. "We are God's *poema*...to do good works which God prepared in advanced for us to do."

Since each of us is God's poem, we can have faith that He has carefully selected each detail of our lives. Only when looking back over our lives will we be able to detect the significance of some of the details, while the significance of other details will remain a mystery until we get to heaven.

God's Love Controls the Details
What do the following verses say about God's tender care being over every detail of our lives?
Psalm 23:1, 6

Psalm 34:9, 10

2 Corinthians 9:8

Why do you think He cares about the details of our lives?

"He leads me...for his name's sake" (Psalm 23:3)—not for mine, but for *His* name's sake. He loves us so much that to lead us is doing something for Himself.

Even though Satan often exercises power, God is still in control. He has set definite boundaries on Satan's power.

What did Paul say hindered him from seeing the Thessalonians? See I Thessalonians 2:18.

R. C. H. Lenski comments on this verse, "Satan succeeded in frustrating Paul's two plans to return to Thessalonica, but only because this accorded with God's own plan regarding the work Paul was to do. Satan has brought many a martyr to his death, and God permitted it. The death of these martyrs was more blessed for them and for the cause of the gospel than their lives would have been. It is ever so with Satan's successes. No thanks to Satan! His guilt is the greater."

Satan may appear to have the upper hand for a time, but to those who trust God to work in every detail, he only appears to be in control. What was Paul's bold assertion in 2 Corinthians 2:14?

Let's consider some of the times God used Satan's worst deeds for His purposes. Read the following verses and identify what Satan did and the glory that God gained through it.

1 Chronicles 21:1, 22-25

2 Chronicles 3:1

The moment we trust God in our situation, Satan's plans are thwarted. God begins to glorify Himself in our circumstances. Our problem is that often we don't turn to Him and trust Him to take control.

What does Proverbs 3:5, 6 say we must do for Him to lead? What does it mean to acknowledge someone?

God does what we trust Him to do. Do you believe a loving God controls every detail of your life? If you believe He is doing that for you, then He is!

According to Evelyn Christenson, prisoners who accept Christ while incarcerated sometimes pray, "God, get me out of this hell-hole." If God doesn't, their response to his refusal is, "If that's the kind of God I'm serving now, I don't want anything to do with Him any more. He let me down."

Frequently, however, inmates who have recently become Christians share that they have already grasped that God knows what He is doing, that it is for their ultimate good, and that they can trust Him completely. Then their response to God is, "Thanks, God, for leaving me here. You have a purpose. What is it?"

A key truth God teaches us through His Word is that when we're living in the Spirit, all our circumstances help us. God can make all things, even others' sins, "work together for good to them that love him, who have been called according to his purpose" (Romans 8:28). What does the next verse (vs. 29) say is God's purpose?

Isaac Watts wrote these insightful words in "The Lord Jehovah Reigns:"
Thro' all His mighty works
Amazing wisdom shines—
Subdues the powers of hell,
Confounds their dark designs.
Strong is His arm, and shall fulfill
His great decrees and sovereign will.

Give thanks that God's plans for You are perfect.

Scripture for Meditation

"God is the Blessed Controller of all things" (I Timothy 6:15 TLB). Read this verse in other versions.

"This is what the LORD says—your Redeemer, the Holy One of Israel: 'I am the LORD your God, who teaches you what is best for you, who directs you in the way you should go'" (Isaiah 48:17).

"Reflect...for the Lord will give you insight" (2 Timothy 2:7). List three areas of your life which you are thankful God controls.

Journaling Time

Space to think, write, pray, and hear God

Are there details in your life that you do not understand why God has allowed? Tell Him that you trust Him despite unanswered questions and difficult circumstances. What does He say to you?

Day 4
Grace to Forgive

Today's Focus from Kikky Williams: I had to forgive him.

After a failure, I was relieved to discover Psalm 146:5, "God takes pleasure in those who...hope in his mercy." Then one day someone hurt me, and I thought I should receive an apology. None came. I prayed for grace, and the Lord lifted my feeling of hurt—except when I'd begin thinking about the situation. How tempted I was to dwell on it!

One morning in my devotions I reread the verse that meant so much to me when I failed. "God takes pleasure in those who hope in his mercy." The Holy Spirit whispered, "Can you be as grateful for My mercy for him as you are when I give My mercy to you?"

Could I delight in God showing him mercy? Or did only realizing I'm the recipient of His mercy comfort me? I began to thank God for His mercy for the one who had hurt me and, with relief, suddenly realized I had forgiven him from my heart.

The Sin of Unforgiveness
Even if someone does not come seeking my forgiveness, I have an obligation to grant forgiveness and extend mercy—even if the person has sinned against me repeatedly and severely. What do you think Jesus meant when He said we should forgive seventy–seven times? Read Matthew 18:21-22.

"Forgive us our debts as we forgive us our debtors" is a prayer asking God to forgive us to the same degree we forgive others. Jesus adds a postscript to this prayer: "But if you do not forgive men their sins, your Father will not forgive your sins." (Matthew 6:15). If any bitterness or unkindness remains, if we do not clearly, fully, and from the heart forgive all men their trespasses, God cannot fully forgive us.

Jesus didn't speak just one time of our need to forgive. How is this truth expressed in the following verses?

Matthew 5:44

Matthew 18:35

Mark 11:25

Luke 6:37

Why is my forgiveness of others a pre-requisite for me to receive forgiveness?

Often only the Holy Spirit can reveal to us those we have not forgiven. The psalmist prayed, "Who can discern his errors? Forgive my hidden faults" (Psalm 19:12). One lady thought she had forgiven her billionaire ex-husband. The Spirit told her she had not because she was still expecting something from him.

I knew my friend had forgiven both her former husband who had been unfaithful to her and his new wife when I learned she was sincerely praying for him to be at peace. The reason? "He was hard for me to live with, and I don't want him to be difficult for his new wife." With God's help there is no wrong done to us that we cannot forgive.

Ask the Holy Spirit to reveal to you anyone you have failed to forgive from your heart.

Sometimes an unthankful spirit is a symptom of unforgiveness. Allow the Spirit to show you any underlying cause for a lack of thankfulness. Is there anyone you could begin to thank God for that you previously resented?

One of my favorite pictures of forgiveness is of Jesus and His disciples eating their last supper. When Jesus announced, "One of you will betray Me," no one could guess who was guilty. Nothing in His demeanor, not even a look of reproach, said to the disciples, "Judas is the man." Jesus forgave and had mercy on all who had part in His murder.

By receiving God's forgiveness through Christ, I am forfeiting my right to be offended when others hurt me. "He does not treat us as our sins deserve or repay us ac-

57

cording to our iniquities" (Psalm 103:10). What would it mean for you to apply this verse as Jesus did?

We knew a man who had been wronged. During this time he hurt deeply, but the Lord impressed him to pray that the man who had wronged him would be effective in his ministry. Miraculously, his bitterness against that man dissolved.

Prayer is a powerful tool to use when we find we're unable to respond with kindness in our own strength. We pray, "Dear Lord, what are You thinking about this one? Give me Your thoughts" and often find we suddenly possess a fresh love and understanding that enables us to deal kindly with a troublesome situation or person.

Being willing to pray for the ones who hurt him was Job's deliverance. God told Job to pray for those three miserable comforters. "After Job had prayed for his friends, the Lord made him prosperous again and gave him twice as much as he had before" (Job 42:10).

Is there anyone who has hurt you for whom you could begin regularly praying?

Why does praying for an "enemy" often bring a willingness to forgive?

Scripture for Meditation

"Be kind and compassionate to one another, forgiving each other, just as in Christ God forgave you" (Ephesians 4:32).

"Bear with each other and forgive whatever grievances you may have against one another. Forgive as the Lord forgave you" (Colossians 3:13).

"Reflect...for the Lord will give you insight" (2 Timothy 2:7). What insights do you gain from these verses? How will you apply them?

Journaling Time

Space to think, write, pray, and hear God

Write a prayer of blessing for someone who has wronged you.

Day 5
What Helps Us Pray?

Today's Focus from Kikky Williams: I had to spend my time in the presence of the Lord Jesus.

A woman of prayer was describing what she had heard in response to the question she puts before Jesus each morning. Her question is, "What do you want me to tell the people?" For many years the response she received was, "Tell the people that I love them." Then one day the reply came: "Tell the people that I miss them."

In the preface to *The Knowledge of the Holy,* A. W. Tozer writes that we have lost our ability to withdraw inwardly to meet God in adoring silence.

Yet God covets our communion! When Jesus told the disciples, "I have eagerly desired to eat this Passover with you" (Luke 22:15), He used an emphatic word for "eagerly desires." In other contexts, the word is translated as "lust." He was saying, "I long intensely to have communion with you." Jesus yearns for our fellowship.

When Barb read the words in a magazine, "Others won't necessarily understand our passion for God's fellowship," she sensed the gentle, conviction of the Holy Spirit.

"Lord, why don't I set time aside to spend with You?" Barb prayed.

To her surprise, she sensed the Lord's reply, "Because you don't expect that I'll meet you there!"

James 4:8 promises us that if we come near to God, He will come near to us. He continually waits for us to draw near Him and wants us to expect Him to meet with us.

Helps to Pray

Satan hates for us to have any comprehension of how much God longs for our fellowship, so he implants thoughts such as, "God doesn't love you now that you've failed Him again." But God asks us not to rely upon our faithfulness but upon His love. "And so we know and rely on the love God has for us. God is love" (1 John 4:16).

When you go into the presence of the Lord, do you think about God and His love? Or do you focus on your feelings and your requests?

In Psalm 136 God's love is the theme. In each of those twenty-six verses, one of God's attributes or works is extolled with the refrain "His love endures forever." Jehoshaphat and his army went into battle proclaiming: "Praise the Lord; for his love endures forever!" (2 Chronicles 20:21). Of all the reasons given in Scripture to praise the Lord, this one could well be the most often repeated! Could it also be the one most easily forgotten?

The Psalmist exclaimed, God "delivered me because he delighted in me" (Psalm 18:19). List three evidences of God's love you've seen in the past month. Thank Him for these.

1.

2.

3.

Jesus told the woman at the well that "the true worshipers will worship the Father in spirit and truth, for they are the kind of worshipers the Father seeks" (John 4:23). Once we understand that God is Spirit, we recognize that our gifts of worship to Him must be from our spirits.

True worship is when our spirit speaks to and meets with God. Through our spirit, we can attain an intimacy with Him.

God will lovingly come close as we draw near to Him. Meditate on James 4:8 and write several ways your spirit can honor that invitation.

Simon had a dinner in honor of Jesus. He had plenty of food for all the guests, but he had forgotten the one thing Jesus wanted more than all else. Christ wanted the worship of Simon's spirit—not simply his service.

A woman slipped into their gathering, and as she stood behind Christ who was reclining at the table, she began to weep. She loved Him so much her tears fell on His feet. She tenderly wiped them with her hair, kissed them and poured perfume on them.

None of this was lost on Jesus. He chided Simon for not showing Him love. "You did not give me a kiss, but this woman, from the time I entered, has not stopped kissing my feet" (Luke 7:45).

Jesus is still noticing those who want to communicate their love to Him. He whispers, "I was looking for you" to those who come to worship Him in spirit and in truth. (John 4:23)

When we come to God in prayer, we're coming to One who is Light. In His light we see light—we gain understanding. (Psalm 36:9) Prayer gives us an opportunity to examine ourselves. What happens if we recognize a time when we've grieved God yet fail to do anything about it?

Psalm 66:18

Proverbs 28:9

Isaiah 59:2

If we have unconfessed sin, we will not desire time in His presence. How often we spend moments, days, even years feeling guilty for a past wrong. According to Hebrews 9:14, why is it possible to be free from guilt?

We have only to look to Jesus' blood and accept His forgiveness. We are as free from guilt as though we had never sinned. "Blessed are they whose transgressions are forgiven, whose sins are covered. Blessed is the man whose sin the Lord will never count against him" (Romans 4:7-8).

In praise we become sensitive to the divine presence. Praise God for loving you so much that He gave His Son to shed His blood for you.

Scripture for Meditation

"Better is one day in your courts than a thousand elsewhere...I have sought your face with all my heart; be gracious to me according to your promise" (Psalm 84:10; 119:58).

"For the generations to come this burnt offering is to be made regularly at the entrance to the Tent of Meeting before the Lord. There I will meet you and speak to you; there also I will meet with the Israelites, and the place will be consecrated by my glory" (Exodus 29:42, 43).

"Reflect...for the Lord will give you insight" (2 Timothy 2:7). What truths are in these verses? How will you apply them?

Journaling Time

Space to think, write, pray, and hear God

If you were to ask the Lord why you don't spend more time in His presence, what do you think He would say?

Day 1
Find True Life!

Today's Focus from Tracey Goss: I realized that I was like the walking dead.

Several times a year when I was a girl, my mother and I traveled sixty miles to the big city of St. Louis to spend a day browsing the sale racks. On one occasion as we returned home with the packages heaped on the back seat, I felt a strange emptiness. Shopping had been fun, but I sensed that life must consist of more than experiences and a collection of objects to satisfy.

God has "set eternity in the hearts of men" (Ecclesiastes 3:11). We were created with a longing for the spiritual world, so we can never be satisfied with the material world alone.

But how can we discern what satisfies and gives us a sense of truly living? What gives real joy and what is meaningless in the end? God wants to teach us to recognize

67

when it is Satan whispering, "Here, eat this, and you will live."

What Is True Life?

God warned Adam and Eve not to eat of the tree of knowledge of good and evil because they would die upon doing so (Gen. 2:17). In what way do you think they died that day?

Jesus' definition of "death" is unlike ours. What did physical death mean in Mark 5:39?

Paul understood this definition of death, and wrote to Timothy, "But the widow who lives only for pleasure is spiritually dead even while she lives" (1 Timothy 5:6 NLT).

According to the following verses, what do people think will bring them a satisfying life?

Ecclesiastes 2:1-11

Luke 12:15

"My people have...forsaken me, the spring of living water, and have dug their own cisterns, broken cisterns that cannot hold water" (Jeremiah 2:13). What are some of the broken cisterns that people expect to quench their thirsts today?

A recent periodical stated, "Most people seek happiness outside themselves—more money, a better job, more sex—

but there's no true contentment unless it first comes from within." The authors state that today's stresses require a "strong, solid sense of self." At first we might think these authors are correct, but Jesus said, "...you have no life in you" (John 6:53). In ourselves we find no life. It's only as He is living in us that we have life.

What terms did Jesus use to promise that the life He gives will be satisfying? See John 4:14 and 6:35.

Physical life exists on this earth where things are seen, but God calls us to a new kingdom where the invisible is more real than the visible. What contrast is made in 2 Corinthians 4:18?

God does not want us to be deceived so that at the end of our lives we say, "I thought what I was doing was real and had value, but all was meaningless, a chasing after the wind." Our spirits hunger for something that is authentic—not an illusion or a counterfeit, but the deeply satisfying answer to an inner craving.

A hairstylist in an elite neighborhood said, "I see these gals come in who live in the million dollar homes in Hallbrook, and I can tell by their body language and what they say that they are not happy. They are empty. If we don't have happiness in ourselves then we don't have any because it doesn't come from without."

I remembered that Jesus said that unless we partake of Him, "You have no life in you" (John 6:53), so I mentioned that without Jesus inside, we, too, are empty. We don't have a life without His life!

What we long to experience is not our own life, but Christ's. "I no longer live, but Christ lives in me," wrote Paul (Galatians 2:20). As we live out God's Word, the unbelievable happens. We actually share in His divine nature.

Describe the qualities of life that Jesus came to give described in John 14:27 and 15:11.

Jesus came to give us life. "The thief comes only to steal and kill and destroy; I have come that they may have life, and have it to the full" (John 10:10).

To the Old Testament writers, a man was living when God the Father approved everything he did. "In thy favor is life" (Psalm 30:5 KJV), wrote the Psalmist. Life, then, to the Biblical writers, stood for spiritual life— vitality, joy, a sense of well-being and satisfaction. What are ways we use words such as "life," "alive," or "living" to also reflect those meanings?

Years ago, I read Moses' words to the Israelites: "Take to heart all the words I have solemnly declared to you....They are not just idle words for you—they are your life" (Deuteronomy 32:46,47). I grasped their implication. If I was to have life in my spirit, I must take in God's Words. I begin to read asking, "What do these words mean for me? How can I apply this truth?"

To my surprised delight, when I sought to express the Word through my life, it became my joy. I felt "alive" when my activities were done in response to Scripture. Jesus had said that if I abided in Him and His Word abided in me, He would give me His joy (John 15:11). When I took in His Word, I was taking in His life. I could agree fully with Jeremiah: "Your words...were my joy and my heart's delight" (15:16).

Scripture for Meditation

"Pay attention to what I say; listen closely to my words...for they are life to those who find them" (Proverbs 4:20, 22).

"Take to heart all the words I have solemnly declared to you....They are not just idle words for you—they are your life" (Deuteronomy 32:46, 47).

"His divine power has given us everything we need for life and godliness through our knowledge of him who called us by his own glory and goodness. Through these he has given us his very great and precious promises, so that through them you may participate in the divine nature and escape the corruption in the world caused by evil desires" (2 Peter 1:3-4).

"Reflect...for the Lord will give you insight" (2 Timothy 2:7). What insights do you gain from these verses? How will you apply them?

Journaling Time

(Space to think, write, pray, and hear God)

Give thanks for every desire you have to feed on God's Word—our "real food and real drink." Ask Him to increase your anticipation to hear Him speak through the Word.

Day 2
God's Love for Us

Today's Focus from Tracey Goss: I hear Him say how much He loves His bride.

"Does God care whether we have pizza and salad today or if we have soup and a sandwich?" a friend asked while we ate lunch.

"God cares about us. If we are greatly concerned about some detail, then He cares just because it is of concern to us."

When tempted to think, *This detail is too small to bother God with,* remember that he cares about what you care about simply because you are concerned about it.

God thinks upon us infinitely. "Were I to count them [your thoughts about me], they would outnumber the grains of sand" (Psalm 139:18). There is a limit to the number of sands but not to the thoughts of God for us. We may at times be unimportant in our own sight but never in the sight of the Almighty.

God's Care for Us

Dr. Kinlaw in his book *Yahweh is God Alone* states that in the Old Testament the most characteristic way of describing the term "salvation" is to say that a person "walked with God."

God has not changed. He is still seeking to have ongoing continual fellowship. Salvation is more than receiving forgiveness for our sins. It involves our daily fellowship with God. He wants us to think of Him as our Friend who is with us and cares about all that concerns us.

How did His miracle of turning the water into wine in John 2:1-11 show His tender concern?

People would not have gone hungry or thirsty without it, but a bridal couple would have been embarrassed. How like Him to use His glory to prevent their humiliation! He, who would go hungry rather than ask for the Father's power to turn stone into bread for Him personally, was eager to protect this couple from embarrassment.

God's love has been described as His desire to impart Himself and all good to us and to possess us for His own spiritual fellowship. Using this definition, finish the following sentence inserting your personal need and your confidence that God will control the details.

"Because God loves me,

All our fears and worries vanish when we discover the love God has for us. The first sentence of I John 4:16 says "And so we know and rely on the love God has for us." The word "rely" means to have faith in or to trust. What role does faith have in receiving His love?

"God is love. Whoever lives in love lives in God, and God in him" (1 Jn. 4:16). What do you think it means to live in love? Why is it equated with living in God?

The closer we get to Jesus, the more His love becomes a reality. Do you allow Him to love you? Andrew Murray wrote, "The heavenly Father, who offers to meet us in the inner chamber, has no other object than to fill our hearts with His love." He invites us to make it a habit during our devotional times to let Him love us.

His love is not affected by our behavior. What might be reasons we have difficulty believing God is always loving us with perfect love?

Twelfth century Bernard of Clairvaux described God's love like this: "In his very essence he is the Lovable One, and he gives himself over, as the object of our love. He wants our love for him to result in our happiness....Such generosity is there in the love he returns to us for our own....To all who call upon him he is extravagant, for he is able to give nothing more valuable than himself....With the refreshing of our souls he busies himself."

Which of these phrases mean the most to you?

Think of yourself as God's child—a much-loved child whose father delights in you and rejoices in doing you good. God is rejoicing over you with all His heart. Why does Satan not want us to dwell on this thought?

Other religions envision their gods as angry and ill-tempered, always in need of appeasing. But we have a God who is singing over His people with joy. Write Zephaniah 3:17 from your favorite version.

God expressed His love when He told the Israelites that His desire was not simply to deliver them from the Egyptians. According to Exodus 19:4, what was the reason He rescued them?

God has recorded what delights him so we can do what brings Him joy. Look up the following verses and write down what God says pleases Him. As you read these verses, consider how you can give God pleasure. Why does knowing these truths help us to pray with more confidence?

Psalm 147:10, 11

Proverbs 15:8

What does Psalm 69:30-31 say about the value God places on our prayer and communion compared to our labor and sacrifice?

The Psalmist exclaimed, God "delivered me because he delighted in me" (Psalm 18:19). List three evidences of God's delight in you. Thank Him for these.

Scripture for Meditation

"The Lord be exalted, who delights in the well-being of his servant" (Psalm 35:27).

"I have loved you with an everlasting love; I have drawn you with loving-kindness" (Jeremiah 31:3).

"Reflect...for the Lord will give you insight" (2 Timothy 2:7). What insights do you gain from these verses? What applications will you make?

Journaling Time

Space to think, write, pray, and hear God.

Read Luke 12:22-32, and listen to these words of Jesus as if they were spoken for the first time directly to you. Pay close attention to what Jesus says about how valuable you are to him. Hear his love for you, and write how it feels to bask in this love. Allow yourself to rest in the love of a God who promises to care for your every need and give you much more than you could ever dare to expect.

Day 3
You Are Special to God

Today's Focus from Tracey Goss: Jesus said, "I want you to marry Me."

God loves us and longs for us with the same intensity that a groom loves his bride! "As a young man marries a maiden, so will your sons marry you; as a bridegroom rejoices over his bride, so will your God rejoice over you" (Isaiah 62:5).

A line from the Westminster Confession of Faith declares, "The chief end of man is to glorify God and enjoy Him forever." We might have thought our main purpose is to glorify God and serve Him forever. But God wants a bride who will love Him passionately.

God's Intense Love for Us

Throughout the Bible, God refers to our relationship to Him in nuptial terms. Write the phrases that refer to the marital bond God wants to have with us.

79

Isaiah 54:5

Hosea 2:16, 19, 20

2 Corinthians 11:2

Revelation 19:7

Revelation 21:2

God is looking for worshipers. We tend to approach Him as though He's looking for workers, but our heavenly bridegroom is wooing a bride, not hiring a servant. Notice in the following references Jesus' mention of the bridegroom.

Matthew 9:15

Matthew 25:1-10

Mark 2:19, 20

John 3:29

How does the thought that Christ loves us as a groom loves His bride make you feel?

We, the church of Jesus Christ, are the Bride, and Jesus is the Bridegroom. Jesus as our Bridegroom wants to give us His love; but He is also waiting for us to return His love. His love is a jealous love. He wants us completely. When we pay more attention to other people, when we give them more time, and more of ourselves than we give Him, He is grieved, because He loves us so much.

Only one thing will satisfy Him—your love. Believing in Him, obeying Him, and coming to Him for forgiveness is not enough. As your Bridegroom, He gives you His tender, most intimate love. What are ways you can give Him your love? Consider new ways to make Him your priority or self-denials that are done out of love rather than legalism.

The most incredible writing of this relationship is in Solomon's Song of Songs. What does the bridegroom declare in 1:15?

What does the Bride say in 1:16?

Jesus desires a relationship with His church that includes both intimacy and passion. He has that for us and wants to develop that in us. How did Paul express his passionate desire for intimacy in Philippians 3:8?

God's love for us is not only intense, it is also unchanging. When two words are frequently linked together in the Bible, it usually means they are nearly synonymous or at least have some special bond. What two words describing God are linked in Psalm 25:10; 36:5; 57:3, 10; 108:4?

The faithfulness of God is "His determined loyalty to a gracious covenant." How confident is God that He will keep His covenant? See Jeremiah 33:20, 21, 25.

"He is the faithful God keeping his covenant of love to all generations" (Deuteronomy 7:9). The covenant He has made with us is not an agreement made years ago that He must keep simply because He gave His word. It's a covenant of love. Because He loves us so much, He is faithful to always give us as much as He can in response to our prayers and trust in Him.

Read the following verses which speak of His faithfulness and record the phrases that mean the most to you.

Exodus 34:6

Deuteronomy 32:4

Psalm 91:4

God will never break the covenant, but He spoke of the possibility of our breaking a covenant He makes with us. The covenant can be broken. God stated this plainly in Genesis 17:14: "Any uncircumcised male, who has not been circumcised in the flesh, will be cut off from his people; he has broken my covenant." (Circumcision was "a symbol for purity of heart and readiness to hear and obey.")

God is seeking a love relationship with His people. No bridegroom wants a bride whose will he has to coerce—either to enter the relationship or to stay in it. He wants a continued love affair.

God desires that from us—a moment-by-moment intimacy. He says, "I will always be faithful and show you My love. All I ask of you is your continued love and faithfulness."

To believe that God makes a covenant with us that we cannot break is to destroy the beauty of our love relationship with God. The constancy of our relationship with Him is like that of a husband and wife who are joined together by a covenant. For the relationship to continue, both must be faithful.

We need have no fear, though. God promises grace to help us be faithful. We do not have to rely upon ourselves but upon Christ within us.

Scripture for Meditation

"Let him kiss me with the kisses of his mouth—for your love is more delightful than wine...He has taken me to the banquet hall, and his banner over me is love" (Song of Solomon 1:2; 2:4).

"As a young man marries a maiden, so will your sons marry you; as a bridegroom rejoices over his bride, so will your God rejoice over you" (Isaiah 62:5).

"Reflect...for the Lord will give you insight" (2 Timothy 2:7). What insights do you gain from these verses? What do they mean to you?

Journaling Time

Space to think, write, pray, and hear God

In eternity the lost will discover they are lost from someone who wanted to live near them forever. They rejected the friendship of One who wanted to give them a place in His throne, the place of a bride. Being the bride means that there will be no closer beings to God in Heaven. Think and record your thoughts on this awesome offer the Lover of our Souls extends to all who will accept!

Day 4
You're a Treasured Possession

Today's Focus from Tracey Goss: He has my name engraved on the palm of His hand.

God declares that you are someone special to Him! "The LORD your God has chosen you out of all the peoples on the face of the earth to be...his treasured possession" (Deuteronomy 7:6). The term "treasured possession" refers to a priceless piece of jewelry—the kind in which a woman takes great delight. After a lady was divorced, she told a friend, "What I miss is being special to someone." God knows we have this need, and He repeatedly used the term "treasured possession" to describe His people.

The psalmist prayed, "Keep me as the apple of your eye" (Psalm 17:8). To keep as "the apple of the eye" is an expression describing the tenderest care. The apple of the eye is most carefully preserved. We are so near Him that it is as though our image is always in the great eye of God.

Perhaps the psalmist wrote that because He knew God had used that phrase to describe His care of the Israelites: "In a desert land he found him, in a barren and howling waste. He shielded him and cared for him; he guarded him as the apple of his eye" (Deuteronomy 32:10).

It was in the place of the most horrible howling of wild beasts that the Lord surrounded His people. The Hebrew word for "guarded" means to surround with love and care, not merely to protect.

God Treasures Us

What is the greatest act of love a person can give? Read John 15:13.

Write in your own words how God demonstrated and still conveys His deep and unchanging love to you. See Romans 5:8 and 8:32.

According to the following verses, of what significance are we to God? Consider John 1:12, 13.

What special names or descriptions does God give to His people in Deuteronomy 7:6 and Exodus 19:3-6?

God has placed within us a deep desire for Himself so we will respond to His desire for us. Most of us do not know our deepest desires. We may know our superficial wants ("I want a new car" or "I want a holiday," etc.) but not our deeper longings.

When Dr. David Benner first met Calla, her longings were all focused on her desire to be married and have children. She was deeply aware of the relentless ticking of her biological clock and felt her dreams slipping through her fingers. She was bitter and miserable.

Calla seemed puzzled when Dr. Benner asked her about her deepest longings. She felt she had told him everything when she said she wanted to be married and have a child. But as they talked, Calla was able to see that beneath what she had thought of as ultimate desires was something more basic—a longing to feel needed, loved, and connected to others. Marriage and mothering held for her the hope of meeting these basic needs.

But her longing was not truly for a man or a baby. It was for love and significance. The love she most deeply longed for was the absolutely unconditional love of God—a love that did not depend upon her performance. "When I desire nothing more than God alone I experience a deep sense of well-being and connectedness," writes Dr. Benner.

The psalmist said, "All my fountains are in you" (Psalm 87:7). The word "fountains" indicates the greatest joy, pleasure, delight. Why could the psalmist say that? Is it a reasonable statement?

Are there people or things you look to for fulfillment and happiness instead of looking to God?

Why is surrender necessary for us to live our lives dependent upon God for happiness?

We must not take purifying our desires on as a self-improvement project. "Only prayer can order a disordered inner life," Dr. Benner insists. Our job is to sit in God's presence and allow Him to purify our desires. Who is the purifier according to Malachi 3:3?

"Examine me and know my heart, probe me and know my thoughts" (Psalm 139:23) is not, as it appears, a request that God would know me but that God would show that known self to me.

Prayer is the place where God transforms us. In prayer God reveals to us our desire and we discover that our deepest longings are nothing other than God alone. What superficial wants often detract our attention from realizing a relationship with God is what we really desire.

If your attention has been drawn to some of your own superficial desires, take time to reflect on them. Face them, naming them for what they are.

What does Matthew 7:9-11 say about His longing to give us our desires?

Scripture for Meditation

"Delight yourself in the LORD and he will give you the desires of your heart" (Psalm 37:4).

"All my longings lie open before you, O Lord; my sighing is not hidden from you" (Psalm 38:9).

"Reflect...for the Lord will give you insight" (2 Timothy 2:7). What insights do you gain from these verses? How will you apply them?

Journaling Time

Space to think, write, pray, and hear God

Have you discovered that your deepest desires are for God alone? Allow God, as you write, to reveal to You what He recognizes to be desires that spring from self. As you wait before Him, allow Him to purify your desire so you are satisfied with Him alone.

Day 5
Go and Tell

Today's Focus from Tracey Goss: Jesus used the testimony of the woman at the well.

With brilliant insight, Alexander MacClaren stated, "Show me the depth of a man's compassion for others and I'll show you the extent of his usefulness to God."

Jesus was a compassionate man. He healed people because He loved them, not simply so they would follow Him. He looked on the multitudes with compassion by showing practical concern to hurting individuals. To the leper who was accustomed to walking down the street and seeing people scatter, shrieking at him, "Unclean! Unclean!"—Jesus not only responded to his diseased body but also to his diseased self-concept by touching Him.

Jesus healed Jairus's daughter, and then in His characteristically quiet but consistent concern, He told them to get her something to eat. He saw a woman weeping over the loss of her son, and moved with compassion, He took the initiative and brought life. When Lazarus died, He wept openly with His friends in their bereavement.

Going Into the World

Many of the people God would have us reach for Him are those we'll meet in the normal routine of daily living. How did Jesus "find" the blind man? Notice the first phrase of John 9:1.

"Those who are led by the Spirit of God are sons of God" (Romans 8:14). As we know this leading of the Spirit more often and more deeply, we will recognize the contacts planned by God. He wants to make His appeal to our neighbors, business contacts, and acquaintances through us, and He cares so much about our good works that He has prepared them in advance for us. (Ephesians 2:10)

Jesus had a heart for individuals. When He wanted to reach out to the tax collectors or to the people in Samaria, He started by meeting the needs of one individual. Notice in Luke 5:27-29 and John 4:7, 39-42 the friends and colleagues contacted because of Jesus' contact with one person.

As we are faithful to individuals, God can reach groups of people.

To whom did Jesus tell the man in Mark 5:18-20 to witness?

What groups did Cornelius call together in Acts 10:24?

Reaching out to people requires an investment of time, love, and prayers. Consider to whom God might have you

92

reach out. What investments will be necessary for you to make?

The disciples recognized a need but their method of meeting that need was not God's method. As we see needs, we must ask for the mind of Christ to know how to respond. Contrast the disciples' solution with Jesus' provision. See Luke 9:12, 14-17.

Why was Jesus solution the right one?

Most of the ideas God will have us use will not be totally new. He may give a desire to share a verse, lunch, or a bag of groceries with a friend. What method did Matthew use in Luke 5:29?

Some of our friends have emotional needs that will have to be met before they can respond to Christ. Jesus often offered encouragement before He offered forgiveness or healing. See Matthew 9:2, 22.

What was Paul's perception of his abilities to testify to others? See Ephesians 3:8.

Paul knew the secret of depending on the Holy Spirit rather than his own abilities. Who ultimately brings people to believe in Christ? See John 16:7-11.

"He has committed to us the message of reconciliation. We are therefore Christ's ambassadors, as though God were making His appeal through us" (2 Corinthians 5:19-20). How do our attitudes differ when we are conscious that God makes the appeal through us rather than feel that the results are up to us alone?

How effective did Jesus consider our words to be to the sinners? See John 17:20.

As we abide in the vine, we will produce fruit. (John 15:5). It is as normal for Spirit-filled Christians to bear fruit as it is for a healthy apple tree to produce apples. A branch on an apple tree doesn't groan, "If only I could produce apples!" Neither does a branch removed from the tree produce fruit. Our fruit-bearing depends on our union with Christ and on our responsiveness to the Holy Spirit.

If we're not being a soul-winner, perhaps we're not abiding. As we bear the fruit of the Spirit, our spiritual lives will be reproduced in others.

One of the reasons we are precious to God is that He will reach others through us. They will be attracted to Him when they see His beauty, His holy character in us. "The nations will know that I am the LORD, declares the Sovereign LORD, when I show myself holy through you before their eyes" (Ezekiel 36:23). Write at least two insights from this verse.

Scripture for Meditation

"For we are God's workmanship, created in Christ Jesus to do good works, which God prepared in advance for us to do" (Ephesians 2:10).

"You are...God's holy nation....This is so you can show others the goodness of God" (1 Peter 2:9 NLT).

"Reflect...for the Lord will give you insight" (2 Timothy 2:7). What insights do you get from these verses? How will you apply them?

Journaling Time

Space to think, write, pray, and hear God

Consider who Jesus might be asking you to reach with His message of love? Write what you believe He is saying to you.

Day 1
Death to Self

Today's Focus from Linda Boyette: I knew I had died.

Vickie and her boyfriend knelt in our family room, asked Jesus into their hearts, and found the joy of having their sins forgiven. A few months later Vickie learned of the need to surrender entirely and to offer her whole life to God.

As she prayed, the Holy Spirit examined the sincerity of her offer. Would she be willing not to wear the beautiful wedding dress she had purchased? Vickie said that as a girl she had not had a lot of pretty clothes, and her wedding dress represented what was dearest to her heart.

It was a struggle, but finally Vicki knew that if God said not to wear it, she would not. With that surrender, God saw she had offered Him her heart's deepest desire. Vickie knew God accepted her sacrifice. She realized later that God had not forbidden her to wear the dress but had simply asked if she was willing not to wear it. Vickie walked down the aisle in her beautiful dress.

Our Personal Surrender

Our natural inclination is to shrink from dying, and we may say, as Jesus said, "If it be possible let this cup pass from me." But those who follow Jesus all the way, say with Him, "Nevertheless not my will but thine."

I was talking with a friend about the need to always please God rather than self. I suggested that when she and her husband disagreed, she focus on pleasing God with her attitude rather than on doing what she chose to do.

"That's hard to do," she said. She spoke the truth. Surrender hardly comes naturally and is seldom possible unless we die to the desire to please ourselves. Yet we must remember that we follow a Lamb, a Lamb on its way to the cross.

In dying to self, we surrender our desire to please ourselves so we can live to please the One Who lives within us. After surrender we can say with Paul, "We are not trying to please men but God, who tests our hearts" (1 Thessalonians 2:4).

If this does not happen we have an ongoing battle. What phrases does Paul use to describe this battle in Romans 7:14-24?

How did Paul state his anticipation of deliverance in verse 25a?

Our natural self wants to say, "Thank You, Jesus, for dying for me. But now I want to live my life as I please, and accept your forgiveness while I have my own way." Paul saw it differently. Repeatedly he referred to Christ's death as being his personal experience, and he says we must allow it to be ours. See Galatians 2:20; 6:14; Philippians 2:5-8.

We may sense the Spirit asking, "Are you willing for me to have that relationship?" "What if I ask you to give up that attitude?" "What if I ask you to speak for me?"

The Holy Spirit is never vague about His requirements. He knows exactly the one thing we must surrender in order for Him to have our all. It is not that He wants to deny us pleasure. He wants to know, "Do you love me more than this?" God knows what our "wedding dress" is. For Abraham, it was Isaac, his much-loved son of promise. God asked Abraham to surrender all his ideas about how God was going to fulfill His promise to bless him.

When Abraham surrendered Isaac, God didn't need to ask, "Now, Abraham, what about that land or those sheep?" God knew Isaac represented Abraham's total surrender. That is always what He seeks. He knows if we surrender what is most dear, we would give Him anything He asks.

Samuel sternly commanded Saul, "Now go, attack the Amalekites and totally destroy everything that belongs to them. Do not spare them; put to death men and women, children and infants, cattle and sheep, camels and donkey."

How did Saul respond? See I Samuel 15:9.

We are prone to be like Saul. God asks us to totally destroy our desires for self, and we do get rid of most of them—enough to convince ourselves we've obeyed. Had Samuel not come along and obeyed God by killing Agag, Agag would have caused great havoc. Sin we refuse to allow God to completely destroy eventually destroys us.

Later, an Amalekite bragged to David that he had killed Saul. (2 Samuel 1:9.10). The truth was that "Saul died because he was unfaithful to the Lord" (1 Chronicles 10:13).

Those Saul was supposed to have destroyed happily reported his death. Saul lost the kingdom and eventually his life because he refused to surrender to the Lord. The cost of not surrendering is always higher than the cost of total surrender. The blessings of God is upon us when we intentionally yield up all to Him.

For us to be a perfect sacrifice to God our whole person must be offered. Every part of our lives—work, recreation, home life, personal relationships, opinions of others, goals—must all be put on the altar. In what areas do you think people find it most difficult to surrender all rights?

The death to self requires our surrender, but it is God's work. What do the following Scriptures indicate our part is?

Romans 12:1-2

John 12:24-25

Philippians 2:8

Jesus humbled Himself unto death, and opened the path in which we too must walk.

Why is surrender necessary before we are filled with the Holy Spirit?

The glorious part of dying to self is that we cease living our self-life, and the life of Christ begins to live in us.

Scripture for Meditation

"Then said Jesus unto his disciples, If any man will come after me, let him deny himself, and take up his cross, and follow me. For whosoever will save his life shall lose it: and whosoever will lose his life for my sake shall find it" (Matthew 16:24-25).

"I beseech you therefore, brethren, by the mercies of God, that you present your bodies a living sacrifice, holy, acceptable to God, which is your reasonable service" (Romans 12:1 NKJV).

"Reflect...for the Lord will give you insight" (2 Timothy 2:7). What insights do you get from these passages? How will you apply them?

Journaling Time

Space to think, write, pray, and hear God

God said to Abraham, "Now I know that you fear God, because you have not withheld from me your son, your only son" (Genesis 22:12). Rewrite this verse inserting what you believe the Holy Spirit would say represents your Isaac. Ask God to reveal to you if you love Him more than your "Isaac?"

Day 2
Jesus, Your Source of Joy

Today's Focus from Linda Boyette: God said, "A relationship with Me must be enough for you."

A friend said that when she was on her way to minister in another country, these thoughts were going through her mind. *What am I most eagerly anticipating? Is it the children I will be caring for in the orphanage?* No, although I loved the children I knew that would not be my greatest joy. *Is it the joy of seeing my dear friend?* No, it was not that either.

As she was thinking on this, the Spirit whispered, "It's the joy of My presence that you are most excited to experience."

She knew it was true. With eager anticipation, she looked forward to enjoying the sweet fellowship of Jesus.

She was doing exactly what Paul meant when he said "Rejoice in the Lord"—not merely in what He gives or does or in what we do for Him—but in His own dear presence.

Jesus warned against rejoicing in our service to Him rather than in our relationship to Him: "Do not rejoice that the spirits submit to you, but rejoice that your names are written in heaven" (Luke 10:20). Our names written in heaven signify our relationship to Him.

Finding Joy in Him

Paul wrote from his prison cell, "Finally, my brethren, rejoice in the Lord" (Philippians 3:1). We must learn to rejoice in God alone simply because of who He is rather than because of His blessings. How do we know if we're rejoicing in the Lord rather than in merely what He provides?

We think we depend on God alone for our joy, not dreaming how much we depend on other things until they are taken from us. When God allows disappointments, it may be so we'll focus on Him instead of what He took away. Can you think of at least one disappointment that helped you draw closer to Him?

The psalmist said, "All my fountains are in you" (Psalm 87:7). His source of joy was in God. Why is our delight in others one of the strongest expressions of our love to them?

One Christian friend admitted, "My happiest moment in life is when I'm sitting on my couch hooking rugs." Nothing is more revealing about our inner man than what brings us joy. Why is finding all our joys in God the ultimate achievement of the Christian life?

How would you respond to this question? My happiest moment in life is when...?

God said to Abram, "I am your shield, your very great reward" (Genesis 15:1). God Himself would be Abram's reward. How was that promise greater than the promise of the honor and riches God could provide for him?

It must grieve God when we view salvation as a ticket to get what we want more than the opportunity to have the incredible joy of His fellowship. An old song titled "Fellowship With Thee" says:

Earthly things are paltry show,

Phantom charms, they come and go:

Give me constantly to know

Fellowship with Thee.

The secret of the deepest joy is living only for Christ, letting Him be all to us. Only then are we truly "in Christ" and His joy in us.

Spurgeon said, "Does the world satisfy thee? Then thou hast thy reward and thy portion in this life. Make much of it, for thou shalt know no other joy."

When Jesus says He wants to give us His joy, He was promising to give us the very exuberance of God! To live with God's presence within us is to have great joy. Do you think a joyful spirit should characterize a Spirit-filled Christian?

How can we have an appropriate concern for the lost and still maintain joy?

To have the mind of Christ is to have His joy. Joy is a choice though. We have to choose to allow our fellowship with Christ to make a difference in our lives. It's not that we're to seek joy; we seek the glory of God, and joy is a fruit of the Spirit as He is allowed to reign in our minds and spirits.

Joy is one of the distinctive marks of those who are "in Christ"—even when in difficulties. "In all our troubles my joy knows no bounds" (2 Corinthians 7:4), exclaimed Paul. Why did the apostles have joy in Acts 5:41?

Do you recall a time of sorrow or difficulty in which you experienced Jesus' joy?

What really gives you joy? Is your joy in God being glorified or in your own glory? Is it in meeting another's approval or is it in the knowledge you have done your best and have God's approval?

Finish this sentence with an unpleasant situation in your life. "Dear Lord, my highest joy is in pleasing You, so it doesn't matter if _____. If You are pleased with me and my attitude, that is enough."

Have you experienced the joy of knowing in your spirit His whisper, "I'm pleased with you"? The joy of His approval is beyond any earthly joy! The excitement of a new house, fame, money, others' approval all seem trivial by comparison. The thing that satisfied Him was doing the will of His Father. Joy, to Jesus, resulted from doing everything for God's pleasure, and He wants that joy to be ours.

Scripture for Meditation

"I delight greatly in the Lord; my soul rejoices in my God" (Isaiah 61:10).

"In thy presence is fullness of joy" (Psalm 16:11).

"Earth has nothing I desire besides you." (Psalm 73:25).

"We have confidence to enter the Most Holy Place by the blood of Jesus" (Hebrews 10:19).

"Reflect...for the Lord will give you insight" (2 Timothy 2:7). What insights do you get from these verses? How will you apply them?

Journaling Time

Space to think, write, pray, and hear God

If we love Jesus with all our hearts, a sure sign will be that He is our source of joy. If you were asked what gives you the greatest joy, what would be your first thought? Tell God how much your relationship with Him means to you. What does He say to you?

Day 3
Give God Permission

Today's Focus from Linda Boyette: I gave Him permission to do whatever He wants.

The early church fathers wanted to understand the Trinity. How could Jesus have been both God and man? How could He be fully human and fully God? Was He more than a man but not quite God? They came up with a word to explain the Father and Son's relationship as being one and yet they each retained their own identity.

They used the word *perichoresis* to describe the relationship of the three members of the Trinity. They also used it to describe the relationship between the human nature and divine nature in Jesus.

It seems that the main characteristic of *perichoresis* is openness. Jesus enjoyed this perichoretic life by being always open to the Father. The result? Jesus was given the Spirit without limit.

Jesus used the analogy of the vine and branches. The branches continually receive their life from the vine. For us to remain in Christ is for us to receive His life as continuously as a branch draws sap from the vine. Just as Christ continually draws life from the Father, so we continually draw life from Christ. As long as the branches stay connected to the vine, the sap constantly flows into these branches. Andrew Murray taught that the sap represents the Holy Spirit.

When we are filled with the Spirit, we become part of this perichoretic life. It is as we continue to draw life from Him that we live. As we go through our day, we look to Christ trusting Him to give us His thoughts and His attitudes.

Giving Him Permission

What are the statements in the following verses from John that indicated Jesus was always open to the Spirit.

5:30

8:28

12:49-50

14:10

The call to live the holy life is the amazing invitation to (as 2 Peter 1 puts it) participate in the divine nature. God invites us to participate in the very communion that the three persons of the Trinity enjoy.

We have no holiness in our human spirit except as God's Holy Spirit lives in us. What does this imply about the possibility of our becoming holy through our own efforts?

What does Jesus pray in John that indicates He wants us to also participate in this perichoretic life? See John 17:21-26.

This continual openness to the Spirit is also described in the Old Testament picture of the lampstand. Zechariah describes the lampstand as being constantly replenished by oil flowing from two olive trees that grew on either side of the lamp. Read Zechariah 4:1-2, 11-14.

Notice that the lamp doesn't need to fill itself, but simply needs to have open channels. The two olive trees represent Jesus on one side imparting blessings and the Holy Spirit on the other anointing our spirits every moment. What phrases in John 1:16 and 1 John 2:27 speak of this anointing?

Christ wants us to be linked to Him so that breath by breath we are filled with Him. It is not that we are to receive a blessing occasionally, but the Spirit desires to have a constant connection with us. Only by receiving His grace through faith moment-by-moment do we have His continual infilling.

This is the secret of holiness. We are not holy within ourselves, but He lives through us. His life shines as love through our eyes, our manner, our tone, our words. Consider how looking to Him to provide our holiness differs from our self-efforts to live a holy life.

How wonderful to have continual direction. God provides this as we stay open to Him. Every moment God is providing all the guidance we need. How does knowing of this possibility help you?

How does Zechariah 4:6 state that our holiness is not through our own efforts?

To fail to live the holy life is to miss out on this incredible relationship with a holy God. God wants us to share in the communion of love that is in the inner life of God.

God is holy and unless we are holy, He can not dwell within us. Good works and our efforts are not enough. For the distance to be closed between us and God—our self-centered nature must be changed so we are comfortable in the presence of a holy God.

What are His promises to change us in Ezekiel 36:25-27.

After He has put within us a new spirit—His Spirit—we humbly learn to rest in Him, respond to His Word, use His strength, and have His joy, and God's holiness fills our spirits.

It is not our striving to be righteous that fills us with His presence. It is His doing in response to our faith and obedience.

Scripture for Meditation

"His divine power has given us everything we need for life and godliness through our knowledge of him who called us by his own glory and goodness. Through these he has given us his very great and precious promises, so that through them you may participate in the divine nature and escape the corruption in the world caused by evil desires" (2 Peter 1:3-4).

"Reflect...for the Lord will give you insight" (2 Timothy 2:7). What insights do you get from these verses? How will you apply them?

Journaling Time

Space to think, write, pray, and hear God.

Are there times in your life in which you desire to be more open to the Spirit? If so, ask God to make you more aware of Him throughout your day. What does He say to you?

Day 4
Walking With Jesus

Today's Focus from Linda Boyette: Our real calling is to walk in a loving relationship with Him.

Dr. Donald Grey Barnhouse in his sermon "The Day-by-Day Christian Life" described his daily activities showing the possibility of walking daily with Jesus. For instance, his secretary brings in his mail. "A swift prayer must be sent heavenward....Every detail has to be done in the strength of the Lord, in a moment-by-moment looking to Him....I have come to the place where I never take one of the letters that is brought to me without a quick prayer to God for the ability to meet the need."

An older godly gentleman told me, "I think most of the time I have the sense of the Holy Spirit's leading. Of course, I tend to pray about most everything."

Remembering to shift our eyes to Jesus is a difficult habit to establish. A. W. Tozer encourages us to "Keep reminding God in our times of private prayer that we mean every act for His glory; then supplement those times by a thousand thought-prayers as we go about the job of living. Let us practice the fine art of making every work a priestly ministration. Let us believe that God is in all our simple deeds and learn to find Him there."

The Daily Walk

One lady said that when she opened her eyes in the morning, she would ask the Lord to open the eyes of her understanding. While dressing, she would pray to be clothed with the robe of righteousness. While working, she would pray for strength for her tasks. And while preparing breakfast, she would pray to be fed with the Word. Throughout her day, she let everything remind her to pray.

Life is filled with distractions that hinder our upward gaze. What does Hebrews 12:1-2 exhort us to do? Write those verses in your own words.

God wants a relationship with us that is full of loving thoughts of Him. What are ways this mindset will be evident in our lives?

Think of your daily activities. During how many of them could you use to help you focus on Jesus?

"As the eyes of slaves look to the hand of their master, as the eyes of a maid look to the hand of her mistress, so our eyes look to the LORD our God" (Psalm 123:2). In the court, the slaves had to keep their eyes upon their master's hand because he would motion to them with just his finger. If they were not watching, they would miss his direction.

One lady prayed, "What do we have to offer You but our attention?" Yet, we often forget God. Why not ask Him to perfect that quality of looking to Him?

We frequently don't think to ask for specific needs. I had wanted to wake up during the night for devotions, so I asked the Lord to awaken me. He did, and I lay there for a few moments and soon was back to sleep. One night I thought of also asking that He help me stay awake. He did! In what areas do you need to ask for specific help?

God delights in giving moment-by-moment assistance and guidance to those who look to Him. Trust and praise Him for the help He'll give today—the interruptions, the help in your work, the interactions with others.

Those who seek Him with all their hearts find Him. And if our seeking includes looking for Him in the ordinary routine of our everyday lives, we will find Him there.

When Jesus said, "I live because of the Father" (John 6:57), He was saying He received His life continually from the Father. This is an important concept, because He asks that we recognize that we, too, draw life from Him moment by moment.

Consider the significance of the present tense verbs in John 4:14; 6:56-58.

If Jesus could not do the work of God except in intimate relationship to and dependence upon the Father, it is certain that our own fruitful life will come as we walk with and depend upon the Father.

How does John 6:63 sum up the importance of the role of the Spirit?

117

What picture did Jesus use to teach the possibility of our continually receiving the Spirit? See John 15:1-8. List at least two ways our life in Christ is to be like the vine and branch.

When Jesus says, "Remain in me and I will remain in you" (John 15:4), He is saying to the degree that you remain in Me, I will remain in you. Our constant abiding depends upon our consistent fellowship with Him.

Why is it vital to our living in the Spirit to think often about Him through the day?

What is the secret of those who have a loving relationship with God? They've learned to make time for God. Often work crowds our time for worship, but for them fellowship with God crowds their work. While alone with Him, they learn to recognize the voice of the Spirit. A couple who has been married many years often need no more than a silent glance to understand what the other is thinking. Gaining a sensitivity to the Spirit will come as we spend much time in His presence.

Jesus spent much time alone in prayer. What were times He set aside to be with His Father? See Mark 1:35 and Luke 5:16.

Why do you think He used His time in that way?

How important to your relationship with God do you consider your devotional time to be?

Scripture for Meditation

"Therefore, since we are surrounded by such a great cloud of witnesses, let us throw off everything that hinders and the sin that so easily entangles, and let us run with perseverance the race marked out for us. Let us fix our eyes on Jesus, the author and perfecter of our faith" (Hebrews 12:1-2).

"Since, then, you have been raised with Christ, set your hearts on things above, where Christ is seated at the right hand of God. Set your minds on things above, not on earthly things." (Colossians 3:1-2).

"Reflect...for the Lord will give you insight" (2 Timothy 2:7). What insights do you get from these verses? How will you apply them?

Journaling Time

Space to think, write, pray, and hear God.

What words would you use to describe your daily walk with the Lord? What could you do to improve it? What does God say to you about how much He values your fellowship?

Day 5
What Is Holiness?

Today's Focus from Linda Boyette: "Fill me with Yourself so I can live with Your responses and Your nature so the world sees your holiness."

To live a holy life may seem as impossible as the idea pictured on a poster of a small sleepy cat nestling inside a box. On the outside is the picture of a tiger. The caption reads, "When you dream, dream big." There is no way that the little kitten will become a tiger-cat without some drastic mutation. God's command, though, to be holy is not an impossible command.

The secret of the holy life is Christ in you—not just Christ for you nor just Christ with you. This is the holy life: the life of Christ lived through us.

Holiness is not personal character slowly attained, but union with the Lord Jesus. It is a joyful life—a life of receiving His love and of keeping in step with the Spirit. If God is holy and He made us to be like Himself, then God has designed us to be holy as well.

God Makes Us Holy

What did Paul state in Ephesians 1:4 was God's design before the foundation of the world?

Originally the word holy did not have moral significance; it simply meant to be like one's deity. If the god the people worshiped was immoral, they followed the god's behavior. "If Baal lies, I can lie; if Baal is promiscuous, I can be promiscuous."

But when our God says He is holy, He is saying that what is distinct about Him is His attitude toward ethical behavior. That is why when people come close to God, their ethics change. Paul tells us that our moral nature should reflect God's when he says we are "created to be like God in true righteousness and holiness" (Ephesians 4:24).

A friend told me that after leading a night of prayer in her church, people who attended came to her home the following day to confess. One confessed to having had an abortion and another said he had mistreated his wife. Such behavior had suddenly become unacceptable. To become holy as God is holy means to be as He is in our ethics and morals.

Holiness means the presence of God. He is the only Holy One, and so anyone who is holy is someone who is filled with the presence of God. In the Old Testament, Moses and Joshua were both told they were standing on holy ground. (Exodus 3:5 and Joshua 5:15) But the ground was holy only as long as God's presence was there. Canaan was not a holy land when it was controlled by the Canaanites; it became the Holy Land when God came and lived there. Even the Holy of Holies in the temple was not holy until the presence of God filled it.

The central role of God's Spirit is to make our spirits holy enabling us to fulfill His command, "Be holy because I am holy" (Leviticus 11:44; 19:2).

Holiness is not an accomplishment but a gift received by faith. Faith is the key word. We trust Him to replace our selfish nature with His holy nature. When we believe that He who promised to put His Holy Spirit within our hearts is faithful, we are made holy.

We then live moment by moment trusting Him to live through us. Rewrite His promise in Luke 11:13 making it His personal promise to you.

Why do you think God's Spirit is termed the "Holy Spirit" and not the powerful Spirit, joyful Spirit, or even the loving Spirit?

I was sitting by a lady at a luncheon and, in response to her question, was explaining God's desire for us to live holy lives. "God doesn't ask of us something which He doesn't enable us to do, so when He says, 'Be holy as I am holy,' He makes it possible for us to do that."

"Oh, you mean He doesn't set us up to fail?"

How true. As Augustine said, "What God commands, He provides." He who has called us to live a holy life has made perfect provision for us to do so.

"But you will receive power when the Holy Spirit comes upon you" (Acts 1:8). What will the Holy Spirit give us power to do when His Spirit fills our spirits?

If the Holy Spirit was sent to give Christians power to live a holy life, why do you think so many live defeated?

If people judge the gospel by us—and they will—what will cause them to believe our Christianity has more power than any other philosophy?

Why does God want us to be holy? See Ezekiel 36:23 and 37:27, 28. Write at least two insights from these verses.

Has God's reason for wanting holy people changed since the Old Testament was written? How is His purpose stated in 1 Peter 2:9?

How does Hebrews 12:14 teach that without holiness in our lives, others won't see God?

What attitudes might we have that would hinder others from being aware of His holy presence within us?

According to John 17:23, what will be the best evidence of His indwelling?

God longs to make us holy so He can be near us. Also we are precious to God because through us He will reach others as they view His holiness in us.

Scripture for Meditation

"You were taught, with regard to your former way of life, to put off your old self, which is being corrupted by its deceitful desires; to be made new in the attitude of your minds; and to put on the new self, created to be like God in true righteousness and holiness" (Ephesians 4:22-24).

"...be hospitable, one who loves what is good, who is self-controlled, upright, holy and disciplined" (Titus 1:8).

"For the Scriptures say, 'You must be holy because I am holy'" (1 Peter 1:16).

"Reflect...for the Lord will give you insight" (2 Timothy 2:7). What insights do you get from these verses? How will you apply them?

Journaling Time

Space to think, write, pray, and hear God.

Linda prayed, "Give me Yourself so I can live with Your responses and Your nature, so the world sees your holiness." Write to God expressing your desire for those around you to see His holiness in your daily life. Give thanks for His indwelling presence.

CPSIA information can be obtained at www.ICGtesting.com
Printed in the USA
BVOW011212190412

288100BV00002B/1/P